Momma's Home Cooking

Home for the Holidays

Wilma J. Miller

*To Betty
From Wilmamill
Aug 2019*

To Betty
from Blakemain

Momma's Home Cooking
Home for the Holidays

Wilma J. Miller

Copyright © 2018 by Wilma Jean Miller and Raymond Miller. All rights reserved. No part of this book may be reproduced, stored in a retrieval system, or transmitted in any form, or by any means, electronic, mechanical, photocopied, recorded or otherwise, without prior written permission of the copyright holder.

All images are owned by the author or used with the permission of copyright holder or the holder's representative.

Trademarked product names appear throughout this book. Rather than use a trademark symbol with every occurrence of a trademarked name, these names are used in an editorial fashion, with no intention of infringement of respective owner's trademark(s). We have no affiliation with these companies.

For my dear, precious La Tonya.
Your time was too short.
I will always love and miss you.

Table of Contents

Preface xi
Introduction xiii
It Starts with Family 1
Remembering What's Important 3
It Will Be Okay 7
Easter 9
Fourth of July 11
Veteran's Day 13
Halloween 15
Birthdays 17
Thanksgiving 19
Christmas 21
New Year's Eve and Day 25
Martin Luther King Day 27
Appetizers 31
    Anytime Appetizers 32
    Spinach Dip 35
    Pigs in a Blanket 36
    Green Pea Salad 37
    Potato Soup 38

    Taco Soup 39
    Easy Shrimp Soup 40

Main Dishes 41

    Turkey in a Sack 42
    Roast Turkey 44
    Simple Cornish Hens 45
    Stuffed Cornish Hens 46
    Southern Ham 47
    Miller Family Special 'Cue (BBQ) Sauce 48
    Me and Jerry's Last Dance Barbecue Sauce 49
    22nd Street Barbecue Sauce 50
    Grilled Pork Ribs 51
    Sunday Marinated Beef Brisket 52
    Beef Short Ribs 53
    Fall Pot Roast 54
    New Year's Eve Steak in Gravy 55
    Pot Roast and Veggies 57
    Simple Country Gravy 58
    Sunday Baked Chicken 59
    Forgotten Chicken 60

Side Dishes 61

    Corn Bread Dressing 64
    Stuffed Cabbage 65
    Sweet Potato Casserole 66
    Creamy Coleslaw 67
    Baked Beans 68
    Black-Eyed Peas 69
    Mixed Greens 70
    Grilled Corn on the Cob 71

Bread 73

Black-Eyed Pea Cornbread 74
Sour Cream Corn Muffins 75
Country Rolls 76
Wilma's Damn Good Rolls 78
Never-Fail Rolls 80

Desserts 81

Sweet Potato Pie 82
Cinnamon Pecan Candies 83
Sour Cream Pound Cake 84
Cool Whip Pie 85
Rum Cake 86
Rum Balls 87
Little Town of Bethlehem Cookies 88
Arkansas Crumble Apple Pie 89
Pop's Easy Cookies 90
Aunt Minnie's Banana Split Ice Cream Muffins 91
Sinful Double Chocolate Oatmeal Cookies 92
Lord Have Mercy Cake 93
Sand Tarts 95
Cranberry Cake 96
Mashed Potato Candy 97
Arkansas Pralines 98
Pineapple Upside-Down Pancakes 99
Carrot Cake 100
Easy Birthday Cake 102
Sugar Cookies 104
Aunt Greeley's Tea Cakes 105

Leftovers 107

Raymond J's Big Turkey Sandwich 108
Turkey Salad 109
Easy Dinner in a Skillet 110

Turkey Gumbo Soup 111
It's a Party **113**
About the Author **115**

Preface

Thank you for purchasing this cookbook. If you haven't done so, check out my first cookbook *Momma's Home Cooking: Delicious Southern Recipes and 60 Years of Sage Advice*.

You can get your copy at http://www.wilmajeanmiller.com or on Amazon. Want to contact me? Email me at wilma@wilmajeanmiller.com.

Introduction

I cannot believe how far I've come.

In 2017, I pulled together my recipes. I spent hours testing and retesting before I published *Momma's Home Cooking*. People have been incredibly kind and supportive. Sometimes, I have to pull a copy off my shelf to believe that I did it.

I've never had a sales job, and I don't consider myself a saleswoman. If I worked on a car lot, I'd never get a car sold, but you get me talking about cooking and you will never hear the end of it. I can go on and on and on because cooking and food are my passions.

I found that the moment you find your passion, you can do things that you'd thought you'd never be able to do.

When I go to California to see my son, I fly on Southwest Airlines. The flight attendants and workers are so nice. They make certain that I get from one plane to the next and that my luggage is always waiting for me. If there is a problem, they don't charge me thousands of dollars to get home.

No, Southwest didn't pay me to say these things. It's just the truth.

I was talking about cooking with one of the stewardesses and she wanted to look at the book during her break. Don't you know, she bought a copy and then she told everyone that I was a published author.

I sold so many that I ran out of books. That was a good lesson for me: Bring more books.

A few years ago, if you had told me that I'd be a published author, I would not have believed it.

Yet, here I am.

This is my second cookbook. We're focused on holidays. Some of the recipes you find here are in my first book. No, I'm not trying to pad my page count. I want this book to give you everything you need to throw a festive gathering for your family.

In closing, I want to thank you for buying my book. Every copy helps me on my journey, and that help is appreciated. In turn, I hope that you and your family make some incredibly positive memories.

It Starts with Family

Some of my best memories come from holiday meals with extended family. I had more aunts and uncles and cousins than I could count. We'd play tag and fish and catch frogs.

My great-grandmother would tell us stories as we sat around her chair. We loved to hear her talk. Now that I think about it, some of the stories would ramble and repeat, but they were always fun and included wisdom that I wouldn't understand for years to come.

As I grew older, my family began to spread across the United States. Many had moved from Newport, Arkansas, to Little Rock, Memphis, Chicago, the Carolinas, and as far as California.

Even when we had family reunions, we were rarely able to get everyone together again. Each year, our family grew and shrank. Relatives died—always too young. Babies were born, and more people married in or couples split.

The distance only made holidays harder to coordinate.

So, I did what I could. Each Easter, Thanksgiving, and Christmas I hosted holiday gatherings at my house with my husband's family. I made sure we had a lot of food and that the door was open, especially to the young kids.

I didn't have a lot of money, but I got creative. I bought meat on sale months in advance. I got vegetables and other ingredients from friends in exchange for splitting whatever I cooked with them. Basically, I did what healthy villages have done since the beginning of time.

My husband, children, in-laws, and guests ate and joked around, and afterward we played dominoes. I recreated what I had when I was a child and couldn't have been happier.

As I talked with people who read my first cookbook, I realized that many of them weren't raised with the kind of gatherings I had. I watched my aunts and grandmother. I learned basic lessons that I could build on.

That's the reason for this book. If you never had family gatherings and parties, you can use this book to get started. The recipes will help you set the table, but everything else is up to you.

Trust me when I say that there is nothing like being with family during the holidays. You can create memories that last for generations.

Remembering What's Important

When I was a little girl, I remember one of my friends rushing up to me with a big grin. She had a secret but wouldn't tell me until I begged it out of her.

"We got new desks for school!" she said.

We were so excited! It was a rare occurrence that we got new anything. It's not as though our school district was poor. We had several factories and companies in our county. We had wealthy, middle-class, and poor people paying taxes. There was money—but there wasn't any money for black schools in segregated Arkansas back then.

New desks were a big event!

We showed up early one Saturday to get the desks in place. The principal and teachers handed out paint and brushes, and they let us personalize our desks. I made sure my desk was the most colorful, and I used all my favorites: red and pink and yellow. I was gonna have the best desk ever. My desk would be so good that it would take me anywhere in the world. My desk would be so good that it would take me to the moon.

I cannot believe how naïve I was. Not much time passed before we realized that we didn't get new desks; we got secondhand desks. The white schoolchildren got new desks. They got desks so good that those desks would take them anywhere on the globe. They got the good stuff.

As usual, we got the cast-offs.

I grew up in the South, and the white men in charge didn't think that black people deserved anything. They believed if we got something—even if our something was old and used—we were stealing from them.

To be honest, I don't understand it. I will never understand it. We all paid taxes. Why not use that money to benefit everyone in the county? Maybe the men in charge thought we were so inferior that any money spent on us would be wasted. Or, maybe, they was so insecure that they had to punish a bunch of kids to feel better about themselves.

Our principals and our teachers understood, but they put on the best show they could for the children and acted as if we'd hit some sort of desk lottery.

They knew that the school district officials in charge would do whatever it took to make our lives hard. Our teachers wanted us to be happy, for at least a little while. So, we took paint and butcher paper and whatever else the black churches and businesses had donated and we made our desks pretty.

Like all black people in America, we did the best we could with what we had.

What does this have to do with your Easter?

Well, your Easter dinner might be a disaster. You might burn the turkey, forget the bread, or not have enough for your guests.

You can't control what happens, but you can control what you do about it. Remember to always make the best of it for the children.

Christmas is not about toys, and Easter is not about fancy clothes. Would you trade your children for Christmas toys?

Of course, you wouldn't. That means that the toys are not important. Being together as a family is what's important.

It Will Be Okay

When I first started cooking meals, I was nervous. I'd just married into a new family, and I wanted to fit in. My husband loved to eat, so he didn't care what I cooked as long as there was plenty of it. Except for my father-in-law, the rest of his family could be demanding.

It's easy to get lost in trying to make something perfect. The perfect food. The perfect day. The perfect activities.

It's all a waste. I learned not to let things like that get to me and to do the best I could. That's all anyone can ask.

So, remember…

1. It's about family. Thanksgiving might be the only time all year that your family gets together. It might be the last time you see certain people. For just that day, put aside all your old hurts and just be together.

2. I keep saying this because it is important. Don't worry about messing up. You will have people criticize the food you give them. Some people are just that small, petty, and rude. You can't worry about them. Brush off their comments and do your thing. Soon, you'll be a whiz in the kitchen, and they will still be small and petty. And at a certain point, just don't invite them.

3. Potlucks are your best friend. Have every working adult bring a dish. Make sure to say good things about each thing they bring and make new traditions. Uncle Joe's cake might always be lopsided, but that's just how he does it. As the kids grow up, they won't be able to imagine a Thanksgiving without that lopsided cake. Trust me when I tell you that you will make a few lopsided cakes.

Easter

Remember your blessings.

When I think of Easter, I think of how hard life can be.

We've all lost loved ones. We've been downcast and sick. We've been so tired that we can't even breathe right.

We've seen the people in our lives go through awful things and we couldn't help them. Not to mention bills and trying to put food on the table.

I read the Bible and I think of all the Apostles hiding from their police. For some, Christ was the only person who'd ever truly cared about them. They felt as low as they'd ever feel. Their teacher and mentor was gone. They'd seen him perform miracles and they thought he'd always be there. He was the Son of God.

They'd never imagined that they'd ever have to continue without him.

The question on their minds was: What do we do now?

But by Sunday morning, when the sun rose, the tomb was open and they knew the long, long night was over.

The Lord is risen, and a new day has begun!

Suggested Menu

    Roast Turkey
    Basic Corn Bread Dressing
    Roasted Corn on the Cob
    Green Pea Salad
    Never-Fail Rolls
    Sweet Potato Pie
    Red Velvet Cake

Other Suggested Menu

    Sunday Marinated Beef Brisket
    Simple Cornish Hens
    Mixed Greens
    Black-Eyed Peas
    Wilma's Damn Good Rolls
    Arkansas Crumble Apple Pie
    Sour Cream Pound Cake

Fourth of July

Freedom should be more than a word.

Independence Day don't mean the same for everybody.

Taking a lesson from the wonderful teachers I had when I was young, I wanted my kids to enjoy the Fourth of July without having to worry about how unfairly the world would treat them.

I'd take the night off from work and make sure we had plenty of good food.

I still remember those July nights. It never seemed to rain, and we always had clear skies. This was back when you could still buy fireworks. Each bottle rocket exploded in bright greens, reds, blues, and whites. We had chasers and screamers and sparklers and firecrackers.

The sounds went on for hours as we watched.

Later that night, the fireflies came out. We used to call them lightning bugs. We don't see them in Arkansas anymore; it's as though their time has passed by.

Suggested Menu
Grilled Pork Ribs
Pigs in a Blanket
Any Barbecue Sauce

Creamy Coleslaw
Baked Beans
Sinful Double Chocolate Oatmeal Cookies
Sweet Potato Pie

Veteran's Day

My son is a US Marine.

We must never forget all the people that sacrifice for the rest of us. If I'm at a store and I see someone in uniform, I buy their candy or pop for them, especially if they're young. I was young once and money was tight.

Suggested Menu
Green Pea Salad
Creamy Coleslaw
Grilled Pork Ribs
Sunday Marinated Beef Brisket
Any Barbecue Sauce
Black-Eyed Pea Cornbread
Arkansas Crumble Apple Pie

Halloween

You only get so many.

I was never allowed to dress up for Halloween. My aunt and uncle were overprotective that way. I do appreciate that they raised me, but I regret not dressing up as a princess or a cowgirl.

The thing I regret is how distracted I was at the time. I worried about my job, bills I had to pay, and some kind of drama at church. Those nights were just one more thing in a long list of things that I had to do.

I implore you to take the time to enjoy every moment with your children. It is so easy to get wrapped up in stuff that is not important. As I watch young people dress up for Halloween, I think of the few years when my children were able to. I made sure that they had the childhood I didn't have. Birthdays and family reunions are times when you really need to stop and smell the flowers. Slow down and take in the moments.

Those moments pass, and you never get them back.

Suggested Menu
Pigs in a Blanket
Lots of Halloween candy to pass out

Birthdays

You only get so many of these, too.

I only have a few pieces of wisdom and advice for birthdays. Each point is important, so here's a list that's easy to follow.

1. You don't have to do a traditional birthday cake. Ask your children what they like or want. Some kids like cakes shaped like Bugs Bunny—other kids want cupcakes or ice cream cake. Junior likes apple pie? Why not do it?

2. If you have a party, get organized. It doesn't have to be a perfect party, but you want to have a few things:
    - A start time and end time; from 2 to 5 is best
    - Invitations
    - Presents
    - Thank-you cards and stamps
    - Gift bags

3. I hate to say this, but put the presents in a safe place during the party. You'll probably invite your children's classmates and it just takes one child to do something they will regret to ruin your day. It is better to have an ounce of prevention than a pound of cure.

4. Take pictures.

Lastly, I pay attention to who your child is. It's easy to think that all kids want a big party and to be the center of attention. That may not be the case. Some young people would rather have a few friends over to watch their favorite movie and eat pizza. I know one kid who wanted nothing more than $25.00 and a few hours at a bookstore. He saw parties as torture.

Don't judge. To each his own.

Suggested Menu
Easy Birthday Cake

Thanksgiving

You own your traditions.

The biggest lesson that you'll learn about Thanksgiving—or any holiday really—is that you own your traditions. I didn't realize how important traditions were until my children were grown.

They talk about Thanksgiving with such happiness. They reminisce about the food and the time with family. I had no idea how much influence I had on the memories and traditions.

In our household, I cooked dressing—or stuffing as some call it. I only cooked it on Thanksgiving and every third Christmas.

I never used boxed stuffing.

Thanksgiving is on Thursday. On Monday, I cooked three trays of corn bread. We're talking savory cornbread, not the sweet kind that you could have eaten with ice cream. I added plenty of chicken (mostly dark meat) to make sure every bite was full of flavor.

I served the dressing with gravy and cranberry sauce. My kids liked the canned sauce (without berries) so that was one of the few things that I didn't make from scratch.

When my kids talk about our traditions, they always talk about the cornbread dressing. It will forever be this wonderful treat that they got a few times a year, and I always beam with pride when they talk about it.

Funny thing, though—now that they have built their own traditions, they've learned to appreciate Momma's hard work.

Tradition is important, especially now. Families get spread out. There seems to be less time in a day and so much anger in the world. When young people are tested, their choice between doing the right thing and the wrong thing can come down to the traditions they were taught and the example that was set for them.

Suggested Menu

Roast Turkey or Turkey in a Sack or Cornish Hens
Southern Ham
Basic Corn Bread Dressing
Potato Soup
Roasted Corn on the Cob
Sweet Potato Casserole
Stuffed Cabbage
Wilma's Damn Good Rolls
Sour Cream Pound Cake

Christmas

Life is God's gift to us. What we make of it is our gift to God.

In our house, Christmas means both religion and family.

We believe that Jesus was born in the little town of Bethlehem. We believe that baby was special in ways that the world had never seen before. We believe that day was the day it all began, and soon, that baby would save us all.

It can't all be about religion. That gets heavy, especially for kids. Sometimes, it's got to be about toys. Do the toys take away from the spirit of the day? I don't know. I do know that the joy on a child's face on Christmas Eve just warms the heart.

I took my kids to see Santa Claus. We didn't go to the mall, where the white people would look at us funny and you could see Santa Claus get cold when dark-skin kids too their turn. I took my kids to the Santa Claus down on Wright Ave where they'd decked out a trailer with lights and trees and holiday music.

That Santa Claus looked like us and made us feel as though we were welcome.

The brother in the red suit played it up beautifully. The kids felt like they'd gone to the South Pole, where all the magic happens.

"You kids do what your parents say. You be good to your Momma. Ho ho ho," he said in a voice that was so booming, you wondered if he was a preacher somewhere.

"Yes, Santa," the kids said.

He probably could have told them to eat dirt sandwiches and they'd have answered with a grinning "Yes."

Well, our job wasn't to teach them; it was to give them opportunities to learn.

To all the people who complain that Christmas is too much like a commercial: You are right. Christmas *is* too much like a commercial. It's all about what you get and how much you spend.

It used to be about the looks on the kids' faces and the excitement that opening a present generates. And how you use that to teach them lessons that they'll need.

"Remember, not every child has what you have. Never look down on nobody, just cause you got it good today," I told them.

"Yes, Momma."

Years later, when I cook and serve food on Christmas, I think about those days. I see kids growing up with phones and expensive clothes. I worry, and at the same time I don't worry.

I know that growing up takes time. The kids that would have eaten dirt back then have learned not to eat dirt. Some of them were born with that knowledge. Some of them had to learn the hard way, but the ones who paid attention know not to look down on others.

Did you know that a manger is a horse trough?

It's a box that people use to feed horses and cows and farm animals. Mary and Joseph (Jesus' parents) were so poor that they didn't have whatever a crib was back in those days. They had to put their child, probably the most important child in history, in a horse box.

That child is in a horse trough today, but it don't mean nothing

So never look down on nobody.

Suggested Menu

Southern Ham
Sunday Marinated Beef Brisket or Beef Short Ribs
Roasted Corn on the Cob
Mixed Greens
Wilma's Damn Good Rolls
Sweet Potato Pie
Rum Balls

New Year's Eve and Day

Raise a drink.

Ringing in the New Year is both happy and sad for me.

I'm happy because I'm able to get together with my friends and family. Most everyone I knew worked a job in a factory or warehouse. Not matter how young or old we were, we all had aches and pains from being on our feet. We all had kids and the stresses that come with that.

And bills. So many bills.

But that was our lives, and we were thankful for the most part.

On New Year's Eve, we could relax and laugh. On that night, we could forget our problems for a little while.

1980.

1990.

2000.

2010.

Each year came and went. Friends came and went.

In the end, I am thankful to have known them, even the crazy ones that brought nothing but drama.

New Year's Day was always a day of hope.

It would be a few weeks before you remembered to put the right year on your checks and a few weeks after that to get going on all the things that you promised yourself you would do with the new year.

I always cook black-eyed peas for New Year's. Black-eyed peas and collard greens were served on New Year's for good luck. Evidently, Union soldiers raided farms for food and left people to starve. I guess if you didn't insist on owning other people then you wouldn't have to worry about starving, but what do I know?

At any rate, the soldiers mistook black-eyed peas for animal feed. So, in "remembrance," people eat black-eyed peas for New Year's.

A more sanitized explanation is that Southerners eat peas and collard greens on New Year's Day for good luck. The peas look like coins, and the greens remind us of dollar bills. Eat black-eyed peas and collard greens for good luck in the new year.

Here are a few suggested menu items. The recipes for black-eyed peas and mixed greens listed later in the book.

Suggested Menu
New Year's Eve Steak
Forgotten Chicken
Black-Eyed Peas
Mixed Greens
Wilma's Damn Good Rolls
Sour Cream Pound Cake
Rum Cake

Martin Luther King Day

A dream leads to hope.

I don't remember what year it was when I truly began to appreciate Martin Luther King Day. I mean, I've always appreciated Dr. King, but I didn't truly understand the need for the holiday until later.

I was listening to the radio while making rolls. I was dusting the dough with flour, and I was irritated. I'd washed my hands and not dried them well, so the flour was like a paste on my dough.

Two women were talking on the radio. I remember thinking that I'd lived long enough to hear not one, but two black women talking on the radio.

The women sounded educated. They fell into home talk a little, but they sounded like professionals. Our community had black doctors, dentists, accountants, and lawyers. The women sounded like them, the kind of people that spoke with some sense. With all their education, they still understood what you meant when you couldn't sound like a dictionary.

Outside, the rain pelted against the siding on the house. The window was open, so the air inside was cool. I'd close the window after I put the bread in the oven to bake.

The women spoke on. It might have been a show about Shirley Chisholm or the Little Rock Nine. I cannot recall.

I do remember one of the women talking about how she was so hurt when she couldn't go to the swimming pool. Well, I remember the start of her story. I don't remember the rest. Did her story have a happy ending? Did she use that anger for something good in her life? Did the bitterness eat her up?

Suddenly, my legs felt like they wouldn't hold me. I sat down on one of stools that I kept in the kitchen. I felt dizzy, as if I'd been spun on a merry-go-round, but there was nothing merry about it. How many movie theaters, libraries, and restaurants had I been asked to leave? People were nice about it, even the librarians at the Little Rock library, but it was still a slap in the face.

"I'm sorry, but you can't be here. You have to go," the woman had said to me. I was a student at Arkansas Baptist College. I had just set all my things on an open table. I was ready to study, ready to do the year right. That's when she came and told me that I had to leave.

I thought that I'd put all that behind me, but it never really goes away, does it?

My heart ached. What about my kids? I had no idea how to keep them from going through the same thing I did.

Thanks to more men and women than I can count, and Dr. King, my children don't have to go through what I had to go through. All the wasted lives. People who would have been great at healing, writing, teaching, or anything, not allowed to participate, to thrive, to even go for a swim in the local pool.

In some ways Dr. King Day is the America's most important holiday. We don't have any traditions for Dr. King Day. Sometimes, it is just too painful.

I encourage you to take time to reflect. Go to a movie, a show, or a restaurant. The libraries are closed, but that doesn't mean you can't go to your local bookstore. They need you more than ever.

Build your own traditions and always, always focus on the positive.

Suggested Menu
New Year's Eve Steak or Grilled Pork Ribs
Any Barbecue Sauce (optional)
Black-Eyed Peas
Mixed Greens
Corn Bread
Rum Balls
Red Velvet Cake
Cool Whip Pie

Appetizers

Don't let your guests go hungry.

One of the first lessons I learned about dinner parties is that you never let people go hungry. Always have appetizers ready.

No matter what time your meal starts, you'll have people show up early and late. Whether you wait for the latecomers or not is up to you, but you should have something to eat for the people who show up early,

Also, you never know when your meal will be delayed. So, it's better to have a tray of something ready to go just in case. You can put appetizers together the night before so that you don't use up precious time making them.

Anytime Appetizers

Here are the only appetizer recipes you need in an emergency.

Always keep a block of cream cheese and your favorite variety of snack crackers or chips. These versions will help you get started.

Smoked Fish Appetizer
16 ounces cream cheese
8 ounces smoked salmon or your favorite fish, chopped
dill (season to taste)
pinch coarse salt
pinch cayenne pepper, optional
garnish, optional

1. Stir together cream cheese, fish, dill, salt, and cayenne pepper.

2. Put in a nice bowl.

3. Place the bowl on a platter with crackers and garnish.

Shrimp Appetizer
16 ounces cream cheese
8 ounces canned or thawed small shrimp
cocktail sauce
coarse salt

1. Place the block of cream cheese on a platter.

2. Cover the block with shrimp. Depending on how you want to present the dish, you can pile the shrimp on or press shrimp into the cream cheese until it is covered.

3. Cover with your favorite cocktail sauce. Serve any excess sauce in a separate bowl. Place excess shrimp on the platter.

Pepper Jelly Appetizer
16-ounce block of cream cheese
8 ounces pepper jelly (any flavor)
1 small or medium container of fresh strawberries

1. Slice strawberries into thin pieces.

2. Spread a thick layer of pepper jelly over the cream cheese block.

3. Add strawberry slices on top of the jelly.

4. Serve on a platter with crackers, extra strawberry slices, and pepper jelly.

Spinach Dip

1 package chopped spinach, thawed (10 ounces or so)
8 ounces sour cream
8 ounces plain yogurt
1/2 cup mayonnaise
1 package dry vegetable soup mix (I use Lipton brand)
3 green onions, chopped
1 teaspoon lemon juice

1. Squeeze the spinach to remove excess moisture.

2. In a large bowl, stir sour cream, yogurt, and mayo.

3. Continue stirring and add soup mix.

4. Stir in spinach and onions and lemon juice.

5. Chill for at least an hour and serve cold.

Pigs in a Blanket

Did you know that some people make Pigs in a Blanket with bread instead of bacon? And they don't use a grill.

6 hot dogs
6 strips bacon
toothpicks
6 buns

1. Wrap each hot dog in a strip of bacon. Use two toothpicks to hold the bacon in place.

2. Grill the hot dog on low heat for eight to ten minutes, turning every couple of minutes. Remember, bacon runoff will cause your fire to flare up. Place so that the flame is not directly on the hot dogs. You can also use a metal container to catch the bacon grease.

3. When the hot dogs are almost done, place the buns on the grill for about a minute, until they have nice grill marks.

4. Remove the hot dogs when they are as crisp as you want.

Green Pea Salad

1 cup mayonnaise
1 small can green peas (4–6 ounces)
1 small jar pimientos (2 ounces)
1/4 cup onion, diced
1/4 cup green pepper, diced
3 boiled eggs, chopped

1. Place mayonnaise in bowl.

2. By hand, mix in peas, pimento, onion, and green pepper.

3. Mix in eggs.

4. Chill for at least an hour and serve cold.

Potato Soup

1/2 cup carrots, chopped
1/2 cup celery, chopped
1/2 cup onion, chopped
3 cups potatoes, diced
2 chicken-flavored bouillon cubes
2 cups milk
1 cup cheddar cheese, shredded
water
pepper to taste
1/2 teaspoon salt
1/4 cup parsley, chopped

1. In a pot, add carrots, celery, onions, and potatoes and cover with water.
2. Bring to a boil on medium high heat and add bouillon cubes.
3. Lower heat and cooked until potatoes are softened.
4. Add milk and simmer on very low heat for 30 minutes. Be careful not to burn or scorch your milk.
5. Remove from heat.
6. Stir in cheese until melted and add pepper and salt.
7. Sprinkle a bit of parsley on top of each bowl and serve hot.

Taco Soup

2 pounds ground beef or turkey
1/2 cup onion, chopped
1 can stewed tomatoes (16 ounces)
1 can pinto beans (16 ounces)
1 can whole kernel corn (16 ounces)
1 can tomato sauce (16 ounces)
1 packet taco seasoning
1 avocado, diced
corn chips
sour cream (optional)
1 cup cheddar cheese or Mexican style cheese, shredded
salt and pepper to taste

1. In a skillet, brown the meat with the onions. Season with salt and pepper.

2. Drain the meat to remove the fat.

3. Add the tomatoes, beans, corn, and sauce. Do not drain the liquid from the cans.

4. Stir in the taco seasoning.

5. Bring to a boil, reduce heat, and simmer.

6. Cover for 20 minutes, stirring often.

7. Add avocado last or serve avocado with meal.

8. Sprinkle with cheese and serve hot.

Easy Shrimp Soup

1 small can small shrimp (4–6 ounces)
1 can shrimp soup (8 ounces)
1 can potato soup (8 ounces)
1 can celery soup (8 ounces)
1 can milk (8 ounces), optional

1. In a pot, combine shrimp and all three cans of soup.
2. Stir while heating slowly.
3. If you like, you can add milk.
4. Simmer for 20 to 30 minutes.
5. Serve hot.

Main Dishes

Always Have a Backup

Your main dish is the centerpiece of your meal. When you throw a dinner party, you can get away with one main dish. If you are new to holiday cooking, cook a second dish... just in case.

Cook a pot roast if your turkey does something funny or have a ham ready if you're uncertain your hens will turn out right.

Turkey in a Sack

1 turkey (14–16 pounds)
1 teaspoon black pepper
1 teaspoon salt
3 teaspoons paprika
1 tablespoon onion powder
1 teaspoon garlic powder
1 cup hot water
1 cup vegetable oil

1. Preheat oven to 325°F.
2. To make a seasoning mix, combine pepper, salt, paprika, onion powder, garlic powder, and hot water in a bowl. Let stand for 10 minutes.
3. Add oil and mix well.
4. Inside the turkey you'll find a sack with the organs and neck. Remove this. You can use it for gravy.
5. Wash turkey well. Rub seasoning mix over turkey and inside. Place turkey inside brown paper sack and put in a large roasting pan.
6. Use aluminum foil to hold the bag closed. You don't have to do anything fancy. Fold the end of the bag down and using a sheet of foil to crimp the bag closed.

With the paper sack you don't have to baste your turkey. If you don't have a paper sack, cover your roasting pan in aluminum foil or use a plastic bag designed for cooking in an oven.

7. Bake in the oven for 10 minutes per pound. A 15-pound turkey will take 150 minutes, or 2 hours and 30 minutes. Use a meat thermometer to check that your turkey temperature is at least 325°F in the breast and thigh.

8. After baking, allow turkey to sit for 15 minutes before carving.

Roast Turkey

1 turkey (18 pounds or so)
1/2 cup unsalted butter, softened
Salt and fresh ground pepper, to taste
1 1/2 quarts turkey or chicken stock
8 cups prepared dressing

1. Preheat oven to 325°F and place rack in the lowest position in the oven.
2. Remove the turkey neck and giblets from inside the bird.
3. Rinse the turkey and pat dry with paper towels.
4. Place the turkey, breast side up, in the roasting pan.
5. Loosely fill the body cavity with stuffing. Rub the skin with the softened butter, and season with salt and pepper.
6. Pour 2 cups turkey stock into the bottom of the roasting pan and cover the pan with aluminum foil.
7. Roast the turkey and every 30 minutes pour dripping from the bottom of the pan over the turkey.
8. When the drippings evaporate, add stock to moisten them, about 1–2 cups at a time.
9. Remove aluminum foil after 2 1/2 hours.
10. Continue roasting until a meat thermometer inserted in the meaty part of the thigh reads 165°F, about 4 hours total.
11. Transfer the turkey to a large serving platter, and let it stand for at least 20 to 30 minutes before carving.

Simple Cornish Hens

Cornish hens (1–2 per person)
Use the following for each bird:
1 tablespoon lemon juice
salt and pepper to taste
2 springs parsley (about a tablespoon worth)
pinch crushed rosemary
1 tablespoon butter
4 strips bacon

1. If necessary, thaw hens overnight in the refrigerator.
2. When you are ready to cook, preheat oven to 350°F and place rack in the lowest position in the oven.
3. Rinse hens with water and pat dry.
4. Sprinkle cavities with lemon juice.
5. On the outside, salt and pepper to desired taste and then rub with butter and sprinkle with 1 or 2 springs of parsley, a pinch of crushed rosemary, and 1 tablespoon of butter.
6. Place a wire rack on the bottom of the pan to keep the birds from sticking to the pan and burning.
7. Place the hens breast side up in roasting pan.
8. Cover the breast of each bird with bacon slices.
9. Roast in the oven for 45–50 minutes, or until fork-tender.

Stuffed Cornish Hens

4 cups wild rice, cooked
6 Cornish hens
Wine Glaze

1. If necessary, thaw hens overnight in refrigerator.
2. Preheat oven to 325°F.
3. Rinse hens with water and pat dry with paper towel.
4. Stuff the cavity of each hen loosely with wild rice.
5. Salt and pepper to taste.
6. Place hen in a shallow roasting pan and cover loosely with foil.
7. Roast in oven for 30 minutes.
8. Uncover, baste with Wine Glaze, and serve.

Wine Glaze for Cornish Hens

1/2 cup wine
1/2 teaspoon sugar
3 tablespoons melted butter

3/4 teaspoon salt
1/8 teaspoon pepper
1 1/2 teaspoon lemon juice

1. In a small bowl, mix wine, sugar, melted butter, salt, pepper, and lemon juice.
2. When ready, use a food brush or spoon to glaze your hens.

Southern Ham

1 ham (12–20 pounds)
1/2 cup honey
1/2 cup mustard, spicy or yellow

1. Preheat oven to 350°F.
2. Stir together honey and mustard in a bowl.
3. Rinse ham and pat dry.
4. Rub honey-mustard mixture over the entire ham.
5. Place in a roasting pan and cover with a lid or aluminum foil.
6. Bake for 2 hours.

Miller Family Special 'Cue (BBQ) Sauce

1/2 cup brown sugar
1/4 cup paprika
1/4 cup chili powder
1 tablespoon onion powder
1 teaspoon garlic powder
1 teaspoon salt
1/4 cup vinegar
1 1/2 cups water
1 1/2 cups ketchup
1/2 cup Worcestershire sauce
1 teaspoon thyme
1/3 cup lemon juice

1. In a sauce pan, stir sugar, paprika, chili powder, onion powder, garlic powder, salt, vinegar, water, ketchup, Worcestershire sauce, thyme, and lemon juice.
2. Bring to a boil.
3. Lower heat and carefully simmer for 30 minutes.
4. Serve as a sauce over meat.

Me and Jerry's Last Dance Barbecue Sauce

1/2 cup chili sauce
1/3 cup Worcestershire sauce
1 tablespoon onion powder
1 teaspoon garlic powder
1/2 teaspoon salt
1 teaspoon black pepper
1/4 cup vinegar
1 teaspoon celery seed
1 tablespoon brown sugar
1 can beer

1. In a sauce pan, mix chili sauce, Worcestershire sauce, onion powder, garlic powder, salt, pepper, vinegar, celery seed, and brown sugar.
2. Carefully simmer over low heat for 30 minutes.
3. Add beer and cook (on low to medium heat) for another 10 minutes.
4. Serve as a sauce over meat.

22nd Street Barbecue Sauce

1 bottle ketchup (about 14 ounces)
1 bottle steak sauce (about 14 ounces)
1/3 cup Worcestershire sauce
1/2 cup brown sugar
1 cup water
1 tablespoon garlic powder
juice from 1 lemon
1 tablespoon yellow mustard
Tabasco sauce (or any vinegar-based hot sauce)

1. In a sauce pan, combine ketchup, steak sauce, Worcestershire sauce, brown sugar, and water.
2. Simmer over low heat for 5 minutes.
3. Stir in garlic powder, lemon juice, mustard, and Tabasco sauce.
4. Continue simmering for 1 hour. Do not boil or allow to scorch.
5. Serve over barbecued, smoked, or grilled meat such as beef, chicken, or pork.

Grilled Pork Ribs

4 pounds baby back ribs
salt and pepper to taste
barbeque sauce (see previous recipes)

1. Preheat oven to 350°F.
2. Rinse ribs and season with salt and pepper (mostly pepper).
3. Place ribs in two 10x15-inch roasting pans. Cover pans with aluminum foil.
4. Bake in the preheated oven for 45 minutes, or until meat is mostly done.
5. Preheat and clean grill.
6. Lightly oil preheated grill and transfer ribs from the oven to the grill.
7. Grill meat over medium heat for 25 minutes.
8. Baste ribs generously with barbeque sauce, and turn every 6–8 minutes.

Sunday Marinated Beef Brisket

beef brisket (5–6 pounds)
2 cans beef stock (8–12 ounces each)
1/2 cup soy sauce
1/2 cup liquid smoke
2 teaspoons garlic powder
salt and black pepper, to taste

1. Mix beef stock, soy sauce, and liquid smoke by hand in a bowl.

2. Place brisket in a pan and pour mixture over the meat.

3. Marinate beef in mixture for 2 to 4 hours, turning beef over a few times.

4. Carefully salt and pepper both sides of the meat.

5. Cover pan with lid or aluminum foil.

6. Cook in marinade at 250°F for 6 hours. For a larger brisket, add one hour per additional pound.

Beef Short Ribs

beef short ribs (6–8 pounds)
1/2 cup oil
1 1/2 tablespoons dry mustard
1 teaspoon salt
1/2 teaspoon cayenne pepper
2 beef bouillon cubes
2 tablespoons Worcestershire sauce
2 tablespoon horseradish
1 cup onion, chopped
2 cups water
salt and black pepper to taste

1. In a bowl, combine oil, mustard, salt, cayenne pepper, bouillon cubes, Worcestershire sauce, and horseradish.
2. Wash ribs and then salt and pepper to taste.
3. Add enough oil to a skillet or pan to cover the bottom.
4. Brown ribs with onions.
5. Pour sauce over ribs and onions and add 2 cups of water.
6. Cover pan and cook on low heat for 2 1/2 hours, or until tender.

Fall Pot Roast

beef rump roast (2 1/2—3 pounds)
1 1/2 tablespoons All Seasoning
1 tablespoon garlic powder
1 tablespoon black pepper
1/4 cup oil
3 cans cream chicken soup (6–8 ounces each)
2 stalks celery, cut in 1-inch pieces
1 onion, cut into small pieces
2 white potatoes, cut into small pieces

1. Preheat oven to 350°F.

2. Rinse meat and season with All Seasoning, garlic powder, and black pepper.

3. Pour oil into a Dutch oven and brown meat over medium-high heat.

4. Remove from heat. Cover Dutch oven and place in oven. Roast for 1 1/2 hours, or until meat is almost tender.

5. Add celery, onion, and potatoes.

6. Return to oven for 1 to 1 1/2 hours.

New Year's Eve Steak in Gravy

2 New York strip steaks (8–12 ounces)
1/4 cup olive oil
1/2 cup chopped shallots
2 tablespoons butter
1 teaspoon crushed garlic
1/2 cup dry red wine
salt and pepper to taste

1. Rinse steaks and pat dry. Salt and pepper to taste. You can also experiment with garlic powder or onion powder.

2. Add oil and preheat a cast iron skillet on medium heat. If you don't have a cast iron skillet, then use what you do have.

3. Cook shallots in oil until tender, and then add butter, garlic, and wine.

4. Cook until liquid is reduced by more than half.

5. Pour shallot mixture into heat-proof container.

6. Increase heat to medium high.

7. When pan just barely starts to smoke, add steaks with room between them so they do not touch.

8. Sear steaks in skillet for about 5–10 minutes, depending on desired level of doneness.

    For medium to well done, reduce heat and add an extra 3 minutes.

9. Reduce heat to low and pour shallot mixture over steaks.

10. Cook until gravy is hot and remove from heat.

11. Serve warm with vegetables and rice or baked potatoes.

Pot Roast and Veggies

See the next page for my Home Country Gravy recipe.

beef pot roast (8–10 pounds)
1/4 cup flour
3/4 teaspoon salt
1 teaspoon black pepper
1/4 cup oil
8 medium potatoes
1/2 cup water
5 peppercorns
3 bay leaves
5 small onions, quartered
8 carrots, cut into bite-size pieces

1. Rinse the meat and pat it dry.

2. Mix flour, salt, and pepper and rub on roast to season it.

3. Heat oil in a heavy skillet or Dutch oven. Add roast and cook over medium heat, turning it to brown all sides.

4. Add potatoes, water, peppercorns, and bay leaves. Cover and cook over medium heat for 2 hours.

5. Add onions and carrots. Recover and cook 30 minutes, or until vegetables are tender.

6. Skim off excess fat. Remove bay leaves and peppercorns.

7. Serve on a platter with the vegetables. You can also serve with gravy.

Simple Country Gravy

1 tablespoon cornstarch
1 cup of liquid from cooked beef roast

1. In a pan or skillet, heat juice from the roast. Use low heat and do not boil.

2. Add cornstarch.

3. Stir constantly and cook until thick. Serve hot with beef, rice, or vegetables.

If gravy is too thick, add water. If gravy is to thin, add more cornstarch.

Sunday Baked Chicken

1 chicken
1 stick margarine
1 tablespoon parsley, chopped
1 teaspoon salt
1 teaspoon pepper
1/2 teaspoon thyme
1/2 teaspoon sage
1 clove garlic, diced
1 apple, sliced
1 onion, chopped
2 cups celery, chopped

4. Preheat oven to 350°F.
5. Loosen the skin around the neck of the chicken.
6. In a pan, combine margarine, parsley, salt, pepper, thyme, sage, and garlic. Continue stirring as you heat to make a paste.
7. Rub paste on the outside of the chicken and under as much of the skin as you can reach without pulling the skin off.
8. Stuff the cavity of the chicken with apple, onion, and celery.
9. Place in a pan and cover with lid or aluminum foil.
10. Roast in oven for 1 hour.
11. Serve with stuffing.

Forgotten Chicken

1 chicken, cut into pieces, uncooked
1/2 pound mushrooms
2 tablespoons butter
2 cans cream of mushroom soup (6–8 pounds each)
1 can evaporated milk
1 cup rice
1/2 package onion soup mix

1. Preheat oven to 350°F.
2. Rinse rice as you normally would.
3. In a pan or skillet, sauté mushrooms in butter.
4. In a large bowl, combine mushrooms, soup, milk, rice, and soup mix. Pour mixture into a casserole dish large enough to allow the rice to expand
5. Place chicken on top. Do not stack the pieces.
6. Cover and bake for 2 hours. No peeking.

Side Dishes

Who's to say a side dish is not a main dish?

My son likes to ask questions to throw me off. Some of the questions are fun, and others are so stupid that I don't waste my time.

He asks me stuff like this:

If you had to eat food from one country for the next ten years, which country would you pick? You can't pick the United States.

If you had to spend a year living in a movie, what movie would it be?

If you had to choose, would you be two feet taller or two feet shorter?

See how ignorant some of those questions can be. The funny thing is that two conversations stood out for me so much that I will never forget them.

Space. My son watches all the *Star Treks* and *Wars* and science shows. I never understood any of it. Give me a Martin Lawrence or Madea movie any day. Tyler Perry got it going on. As soon as some alien monster with a butt on its head gets on the screen, I get lost. None of it makes sense to me.

I can't remember what question he asked, but my son says that he'd go into space in a heartbeat. He'd do it for free. Again, that makes no sense to me. Why go up to the moon or Mars or Venus when you could die?

The other questions were almost as silly:

Is macaroni and cheese a side dish or a main dish?

Any fool knows the answer. Then again, some of his questions were made to trap you. Let's go back to this question:

If you had to eat food from one country for the next ten years, which country would you pick? You can't pick the United States.

You say Mexican and for the next ten years all the meat you eat is spicy. Don't get me wrong, I like real Mexican food, but for ten years? Same goes for Italian, Canadian, Jamaican. All the food is good, but unless you were raised on it, you will get bored.

I'm used to eating different kinds of food with soups and salads, vegetables and meats, and so on.

You know what his answer was? Chinese.

He said that Chinese food has rice and noodles and BBQ and smoked meat and salads and seafood. Some of it is spicy and some mild. It has fried chicken wings that I'm used to and lamb stew. There is even a kind of dumpling that has hot soup inside it. The flavor just lights up your mouth. They call them Xiaolongbao. Don't ask me how to pronounce it.

See how tricky that question was. China is so big and has been around so long that it has a huge menu. If you can think of a better answer, let me know. I'd be glad to throw it at him.

As far as mac and cheese goes, it's a side dish. You know that some people think it's a main. They cook mac and cheese and that's dinner.

I guess to each his own.

Those questions make time pass. Next thing you know, the four-hour car ride is over and you pull into the hotel to start your vacation.

Corn Bread Dressing

1 cup onion, chopped
3/4 cup celery, chopped
1 cup green bell pepper, chopped
1/2 cup butter
5 cups corn bread, crumbled
1 cup toasted white bread, crumbled
4 eggs, beaten
1 tablespoon poultry seasoning
1 tablespoon sage
2 quarts chicken broth
salt and pepper to taste

1. Preheat oven to 350°F.

2. Sauté onion, celery, and bell pepper in butter until tender.

3. In a separate pan, warm chicken broth. Do not boil.

4. In a large bowl, use a large wooden spoon or spatula to mix corn bread and white bread and then add cooked vegetables.

5. Stir in beaten eggs and add poultry seasoning and sage.

6. Mix with warm chicken broth.

7. Place in large pan.

8. Bake in oven for 1 hour, or until done. I like to bake my dressing for 1 hour, covered for 30 minutes and then uncovered for 30 minutes, to give it a good brown color.

Stuffed Cabbage

10 large cabbage leaves
1 1/2 pound ground beef
Salt and pepper to taste
2/3 cup bread crumbs
1 cup milk
2 eggs, slightly beaten
1/4 cup onion, chopped
1/2 cup bell pepper, chopped
1 can stewed tomatoes (4–6 ounces)
1 can tomato sauce (10–12 ounces)

1. Boil cabbage leaves in water for 2–3 minutes to soften the leaves and set aside. This will soften the leaves.

2. Preheat oven to 350°F.

3. In a large bowl, combine ground beef with salt and pepper.

4. Add bread crumbs, milk, eggs, onion, bell pepper, and stewed tomatoes.

5. Spoon generous helpings of beef mixture into cabbage leaves and roll up. I usually roll leaves lengthwise. It doesn't have to be perfect. You'll cover it with sauce anyway.

6. Place the rolled leaves into a pan with the seam sides down.

7. Cover the cabbage rolls with tomato sauce.

8. Bake for 1 hour.

Sweet Potato Casserole

3 cups sweet potatoes, cooked and mashed
1 1/2 cups milk
1/2 cup sugar
1 teaspoon vanilla
3/4 cup butter
2 eggs, beaten

Casserole Topping

1/2 cup butter
1/2 cup flour
1 cup brown sugar
1 cup nuts

1. Preheat oven to 350°F.
2. In a large bowl, mix sweet potatoes and milk.
3. Continue to mix and add sugar, vanilla, butter, and eggs.
4. Pour into a greased 9x13-inch dish.
5. For the topping, carefully melt butter in a pan or microwave and stir in brown sugar, flour, and nuts.
6. Sprinkle topping over the potato mixture.
7. Cover with lid or aluminum foil and bake for 25 minutes.

Creamy Coleslaw

1 small can evaporated milk
1/4 cup vinegar
1/4 cup sugar
1/2 teaspoon celery seeds
1/2 teaspoon black pepper
3/4 cup mayonnaise
3 1/2 cups shredded cabbage
3/4 cup shredded carrots
1/2 cup celery, diced (optional)

1. Stir together, milk, vinegar, sugar, celery seeds, pepper, and mayonnaise.
2. In a separate bowl, toss cabbage, carrots, and celery.
3. Pour evaporated milk over cabbage, mix well, and chill.

Baked Beans

1 large can pork 'n' beans (30 ounces or so)
1 cup ketchup
1/2 cup brown sugar
1/4 cup maple syrup
1 medium onion, chopped
smoked sausage (1/4 pound)
1 jalapeño pepper, chopped
1 teaspoon liquid smoke
1 tablespoon Worcestershire sauce

1. Preheat oven to 350°F.

2. In a large bowl, combine pork 'n' beans, ketchup, sugar, syrup, onion, sausage, and pepper.

3. Add liquid smoke and Worcestershire sauce.

4. Place in baking dish and cook for 1 hour.

Black-Eyed Peas

4 cups fresh or frozen black-eyed peas
4 slices bacon
1 cup diced ham, cooked (optional)
1 large onion, chopped
1 stalk celery, diced
4 garlic cloves, minced
water
1/2 teaspoon salt
1/4 teaspoon ground black pepper

If you are using fresh peas, soak them in hot water. To do this, place the peas in a pot, cover them with water, and bring the pot to a boil.

Remove from heat and cover. Allow peas to soak for 60–90 minutes and drain.

1. In a 5-quart pot, cook bacon until done but not crisp. Remove bacon and set aside on a paper towel.

2. In the bacon renderings, cook ham, onion, and celery.

3. Add garlic and cook for 1 minute.

4. Crumble bacon and add to the pot.

5. Add peas and stir.

6. Slowly add water until peas are covered.

7. Partially cover and simmer over low to medium heat for 1 to 1 1/2 hours.

   Serve with corn bread.

Mixed Greens

4 pounds of mixed greens (turnip, collard, or mustard greens)
5 cups water
1/2 teaspoon black pepper
1/3 pound salt pork or ham hocks
3 tablespoons vinegar
1 tablespoon allspice

1. Remove the thickest part of the stems and discolored spots from greens.
2. Wash the greens in a sink or large container of cold water. Repeat until sand and dirt no longer appear in the water.
3. Tear or cut greens into reasonably bite-size pieces.
4. Pour water into a large pot and bring to a boil.
5. Add pepper, meat, vinegar, and allspice and return the pot to a boil.
6. Add greens and cook over medium heat for about 2 hours.

Grilled Corn on the Cob

6–10 ears corn
butter
salt and pepper to taste

1. Remove the silks (the yellow hair) from each cob and, if necessary, remove the stems from the bottom.

2. Individually wrap each corn cob in aluminum foil. You don't have to use foil, but the husks will blacken if you don't.

3. Place the corn cobs on the grill with space between each.

4. Grill corn for 25 to 30 minutes, turning every five minutes.

5. Take the corn off the grill and allow to cool.

6. Remove foil and husks.

7. Serve hot with butter, salt, and pepper.

Bread

Nothing like a hot bread from the oven.

Let's be honest: you don't always have time to make fresh bread. Don't be afraid or ashamed to buy grocery store rolls and pop them in the oven.

Seriously, as you get better at putting holiday meals together, you'll be able to knock out a pan of rolls or a skillet of corn bread like it was nothing.

When you're starting out, you'll have to do some scrabbling to get it right. Trust me, it all works out.

It works out even better if you serve good butter with your bread.

Black-Eyed Pea Cornbread

Here's one of the more popular recipes from my first cookbook. There's nothing like black-eyed pea cornbread and ... well, black-eyed peas. The black-eyed pea recipe is in the New Year's Eve section.

2 cups cornmeal
1/2 teaspoon salt
1/2 teaspoon baking soda
1 cup buttermilk
1 pound pork sausage, cooked
1 can creamed corn
1 cup black-eyed peas, cooked or canned
1 small jar pimientos, chopped
1/2 cup cooking oil
1 small can green chilies
2 eggs
1 cup American or cheddar cheese, shredded

1. Preheat oven to 350° F.

2. Grease a casserole pan or cast-iron skillet.

3. In a large bowl, mix cornmeal, salt, baking soda, buttermilk, pork sausage, creamed corn, peas, pimentos, oil, and chilies.

4. Add eggs and cheese while mixing until all ingredients are thoroughly blended.

5. Pour into greased pan.

6. Bake for 40 minutes.

Sour Cream Corn Muffins

1 cup sour cream
1 large package corn muffin mix (15–18 ounces total)
2 eggs
1 cup butter

1. Preheat oven to 300°F.

2. In a large mixing bowl, combine sour cream, corn muffin mix, eggs, and butter.

3. Pour into muffin pan. Remember that muffins expand, so you don't need to completely fill each cup.

4. Bake for 30 minutes, or until golden brown.

Country Rolls

2 packets dry yeast (each packet is about 1/4 ounce)
2 cups lukewarm water (1/2 cup is used for yeast)
1 cup shortening
3/4 cup sugar
2 eggs, beaten
1 teaspoon salt
6 cups flour

1. In a container, pour yeast into 1/2 cup of water. When yeast bubbles, stir with a spoon and set aside.

   If the yeast does not bubble, it means that your yeast is not active. Discard and try again.

2. In a sauce pan, melt and combine shortening and sugar.

3. In a bowl, add the shortening mixture, eggs, and salt and mix well.

4. Add the yeast mixture and 1 1/2 cups of lukewarm water. Stir until blended.

5. Using a mixer, add flour one cup at a time until you create a dough.

6. Shape by hand into a large ball, cover with a damp towel, and set in a warm place. Allow dough to rise until doubled in size (at least 3 hours, but overnight is best).

7. Grease a 9x13-inch pan.

8. Shape dough into 3-inch balls and arrange in pan.

9. With the bottom of a drinking glass, gently flatten each ball to the size of an American biscuit.

10. Set aside. Again, allow dough to rise until doubled in size (at least 3 hours).
11. Preheat oven to 350°F.
12. Bake for 15 minutes, or until golden brown.

Wilma's Damn Good Rolls

2 packets dry yeast (each packet is about 1/4 ounce)
1/2 cup lukewarm water for yeast
1 cup milk
1 cup butter-flavored shortening
2 eggs, beaten
3/4 cups sugar
1 teaspoon salt
1 cup water
7 1/2 cups flour

1. In a container, pour yeast into 1/2 cup of water. When yeast bubbles, stir with a spoon and set aside.

   If the yeast does not bubble, it means that your yeast is not active. Discard and try again.

2. In a sauce pan, scald milk. To do this, bring milk almost to boiling, then remove from heat and stir in shortening.

3. In a large bowl, combine eggs and sugar until blended.

4. Add salt and 1 cup water. Stir in yeast mixture.

5. Slowly add milk mixture, stirring.

6. Using a large mixer, blend together while adding flour one cup at a time. Mix until you create dough.

7. Shape by hand into a large ball, cover with a damp towel, and set in a warm place. Allow dough to rise until doubled in size (at least 3 hours, but overnight is best).

8. Grease a 9x13-inch pan.
9. Shape dough into 3-inch balls and arrange in pan.
10. With the bottom of a drinking glass, gently flatten each ball to the size of an American biscuit.
11. Set aside. Again, allow dough to rise until doubled in size (at least 3 hours).
12. Preheat oven to 350°F.
13. Bake for 15 minutes, or until golden brown.

Never-Fail Rolls

1 packet dry yeast (about 1/4 ounce)
1 cup lukewarm water
2 eggs
1/2 cup sugar
1 teaspoon salt
1/2 cup butter
4 1/2 cups flour

1. In a container, pour yeast into 1/2 cup of water. When yeast bubbles, stir with a spoon and set aside.

    If the yeast does not bubble, it means that your yeast is not active. Discard and try again.

2. In a large bowl, combine eggs, sugar, salt, butter, yeast mixture, and flour to make dough. Stir until smooth.

3. Shape by hand into a large ball, cover with a damp towel, and set in a warm place. Allow dough to rise until doubled in size (at least 3 hours, but overnight is best).

4. Grease a 9x13-inch pan.

5. Shape dough into 3-inch balls and arrange in pan.

6. With the bottom of a drinking glass, gently flatten each ball to the size of an American biscuit.

7. Set aside. Again, allow dough to rise until doubled in size (at least 3 hours).

8. Preheat oven to 350°F.

9. Bake for 15 minutes, or until golden brown.

Desserts

Who doesn't have a sweet tooth?

I've read several books, reviewed articles, and watched lots of cooking shows. Something that I've noticed is that people don't want to have too much food on hand. I constantly hear people saying, "No, don't bring that. We'll have too much food!"

It might be that I grew up in the South during Jim Crow, when food was scarce and there wasn't always something good to celebrate. I mean, how could having lots of food be a bad thing?

Don't get me wrong. I don't want to waste food. On the other hand, holidays are celebrations. It's not as though we're feasting every week or even every month.

Why limit your good time? How much difference does one more cake make? To be honest, my husband and kids had no problem making any amount of food I made disappear. Plus, I had more family and friends coming by, so I chose to have a place at my table for them.

And I always had a piece of cake or slice of pie waiting.

Sweet Potato Pie

2 cups sweet potatoes, cooked and mashed
1 cup brown sugar
1 1/2 teaspoon cinnamon
1/4 teaspoon salt
2 eggs
1 teaspoon nutmeg
1 cup milk
1/2 cup butter
1 deep-dish pie crust, uncooked (at least 8 inches)

1. Preheat oven to 350°F.
2. In a large bowl, use a mixer to combine the following ingredients: sweet potatoes, sugar, cinnamon, salt, eggs, nutmeg, milk, and butter.
3. Pour into pie crust.
4. Bake on top rack for 1 hour, or until pie is firm.

   Cool for 30 minutes before slicing.

Cinnamon Pecan Candies

1/4 cup evaporated milk
1 cup sugar
1/2 teaspoon cinnamon
2 tablespoons water
1/2 teaspoon vanilla
3 cups pecans, shelled

1. Mix milk, sugar, cinnamon, water, and vanilla in a medium-size sauce pan.
2. Dissolve over medium heat.
3. Add pecans and cook until all the liquid sticks to the pecans.
4. Pour onto wax paper and separate after candy cools.

Sour Cream Pound Cake

3 cups sugar
2 sticks butter (about 1 cup)
6 eggs
3 cups flour
1/2 teaspoon baking powder
1/4 teaspoon baking soda
1 cup sour cream
1 teaspoon vanilla flavor
1 teaspoon lemon flavor

1. Preheat oven to 325°F.

2. Blend sugar, butter, and eggs (one at a time).

3. Slowly add flour.

4. Continue by adding baking powder, baking soda, sour cream, vanilla flavor, and lemon flavor.

5. Pour into a greased and floured tube pan.

6. Bake for 45 minutes or 1 hour.

Cool Whip Pie

1 deep-dish pie crust, baked (at least 8 inches)
2 bananas, sliced
1 medium container Cool Whip
1 stick cream cheese (about 4 ounces)
1/2 cup sugar
1 can strawberry or cherry pie filling (8 ounces)

1. Follow the package instructions to bake the pie crust and let it cool.

2. Line the bottom of the pie crust with banana slices.

3. Mix Cool Whip, cream cheese, and sugar. Beat well.

4. Pour mixture over bananas and top with pie filling.

5. Chill for one hour.

Rum Cake

1 box yellow cake mix
1 small box vanilla pudding mix
1/2 cup vegetable oil
1/2 cup dark rum
1/2 cup water
5 eggs

1. Preheat oven to 325°F.

2. Combine cake mix, pudding mix, oil, rum, and water.

3. Mix well and pour into a well-greased Bundt pan.

4. Bake for 1 hour, or until done.

Rum Cake Glaze

1/2 cup butter
1/4 cup water
1 cup white sugar
1/2 cup dark rum

1. In a sauce pan, combine butter, water, and sugar and bring to a boil.

2. Stir constantly and boil for about 5 minutes.

3. Remove from the heat and stir in rum.

4. Punch 1-inch-deep holes in the cake and pour glaze in the hole and on the surface.

Rum Balls

2 1/2 tablespoons cocoa
1 cup powdered sugar (plus more for dusting)
1/4 cup light rum (use 1/3 cup for stronger taste)
1/3 cup corn syrup
2 cups vanilla wafers, crushed
1 cup pecans or walnuts, finely chopped

1. In a large bowl, stir cocoa and powdered sugar together.
2. One at a time, mixing well after each, add rum, syrup, wafers, and nuts. Use your hands when mixture becomes too difficult to stir.
3. Form into small balls (slightly smaller than a golf ball) and roll in the powdered sugar.
4. Place in an uncovered pan for at least 1 1/2 hours or overnight.
5. Store in an airtight container.

Little Town of Bethlehem Cookies

2 egg whites
pinch salt
3/4 cup sugar
1 cup chocolate chips
1 cup pecans or walnuts, chopped

1. Preheat oven to 350°F.

2. Crack eggs and remove the yolks. (I use the yolks for breakfast scrambles the next morning.)

3. In a large bowl, beat egg whites until foamy.

4. Add salt and gradually add sugar while beating until peaks form.

5. Using a spatula, fold in chocolate chips and nuts.

6. Use a teaspoon to drop on a greased cookie sheet.

7. Put in preheated oven and immediately turn off heat. Allow the oven to slowly bake cookies overnight. Do not peak.

8. This will make approximately 3 dozen.

Arkansas Crumble Apple Pie

1 cup apple pie filling or 5 apples, peeled, cored, and sliced
1 deep-dish pie crust, unbaked
1/4 cup white sugar
1/4 cup brown sugar
3/4 cup flour
3/4 teaspoon ground cinnamon
1/2 teaspoon nutmeg
8 tablespoons butter

1. Preheat oven to 350°F.

2. Pour apple filling into an unbaked pie crust.

    If you're using fresh apples, place the apples in the pie crust and sprinkle with an extra 1/4 cup white sugar and 3/4 teaspoon ground cinnamon.

3. In a bowl, combine white sugar, brown sugar, and flour.

4. Stir in cinnamon and nutmeg.

5. Cut butter into slices and stir into mixture until crumbly. Add additional butter if necessary.

6. Sprinkle over apples.

7. Bake for 40 minutes, or until top is lightly browned.

Pop's Easy Cookies

1 cup chunky peanut butter
1 cup sugar
1 egg
1/2 teaspoon vanilla

1. Preheat oven to 350°F.
2. In a large bowl, combine peanut butter, sugar, egg, and vanilla.
3. Use a teaspoon to drop on ungreased cookie sheet. Allow room for cookies to spread without touching each other.
4. Bake for 10–15 minutes.

Aunt Minnie's Banana Split Ice Cream Muffins

You can use any flavor ice cream that you like. What's your favorite? Strawberry, black walnut, etc.?

This recipe makes about 24 cupcakes.

2 1/2 cup self-rising flour
2 cups ice cream, softened (banana split)

1. Preheat oven to 350°F.
2. In a large bowl, use a spatula to blend flour and ice cream.
3. Place liners in cupcake pan and even pour batter into cups.
4. Bake 15-20 minutes until done.

Sinful Double Chocolate Oatmeal Cookies

1 cup butter, softened
3/4 cup brown sugar
2 eggs
1/4 cup milk
1 teaspoon vanilla
1/2 cup flour
1/3 cup cocoa
1/2 teaspoon baking soda
1/4 teaspoon salt
2 1/2 cups old-fashioned oatmeal
1 cup raisins
1 cup semisweet chocolate pieces

1. Preheat oven to 350°F.

2. In a large mixer bowl, beat butter and sugar.

3. Add eggs, milk, and vanilla. Mix well. Then add flour, cocoa, baking soda, and salt sifted together.

4. Blend until smooth. Stir in oatmeal, raisins, and chocolate pieces.

5. Use a teaspoon to drop onto a well-greased cookie sheet.

6. Bake for 10–12 minutes.

Lord Have Mercy Cake

1 box yellow cake mix
1/2 cup milk
1/2 cup vegetable oil
1 container sour cream (about 8 ounces)
1 box instant vanilla pudding (4–6 ounces)
4 eggs
1/2 cup butter
1 package sweet chocolate chip (about 8 ounces)
3/4 cup German chocolate, grated

1. Preheat oven to 350°F.

2. Using a mixer, combine cake mix, milk, oil, sour cream, pudding, eggs, and butter.

3. When blended well, add chocolate chips and German chocolate.

4. Pour into a greased and floured tube pan or Bundt pan.

5. Bake for 1 hour, or until done.

Lord Have Mercy Cake Icing

1 cup sugar
1/2 heavy cream
1/4 cup butter
3 eggs
1 cup pecans, chopped
1 cup angel flake coconut

1. Crack eggs and remove yolk. Use the egg white for breakfast in the morning.

2. In a large bowl, combine sugar, cream, butter, and egg yolks until the mixture thickens.

3. Add pecans and coconut.
4. Blend well.
5. Cover low heat until icing thickens.
6. Cool and spread over cake.

Sand Tarts

1 cup butter
2 1/2 cups flour (3/4 for rolling and 3/4 for batter)
1 1/2 cups of powdered sugar
1 teaspoon ice water
3/4 cup pecans or walnuts, chopped

1. Preheat oven to 350°F.
2. In a bowl, combine butter, flour, and 3/4 cups of sugar.
3. Continue to stir and add ice water and nuts.
4. Use a teaspoon to drop onto a well-greased baking sheet.
5. Bake for 10–12 minutes.
6. Roll in the rest of the powdered sugar while hot and place on a large serving platter.

Cranberry Cake

2 1/2 cups flour
1 1/4 cups sugar
1 teaspoon salt
1/2 teaspoon baking soda
1 teaspoon baking powder
1 cup dates, chopped
1 cup dried cranberries
1 1/2 cups pecans or walnuts, chopped
3 orange rinds, grated
3 eggs, beaten
1 cup buttermilk
1 cup vegetable oil

1. Preheat oven to 350°F.

2. Sift flour with sugar, salt, baking soda, and baking powder.

3. Mix dates, cranberries, nuts, and orange rinds with dry ingredients.

4. Combine beaten eggs with buttermilk and oil and add to flour and fruit mixture.

5. Mix thoroughly and pour into a greased Bundt pan.

6. Bake for 1 hour.

Mashed Potato Candy

1 cup mashed potatoes
4 cups powdered sugar
4 cups shredded coconut
2 teaspoons vanilla
1/2 teaspoon salt
8 squares baking chocolate

1. Mix potatoes and powdered sugar and then stir in coconut, vanilla, and salt.

2. Blend well and place in a large 9x13-inch dish in a layer about 1/2 inch thick.

3. In a double boiler, melt chocolate over hot water.

4. Drizzle chocolate over candy.

5. Cool overnight in the refrigerator and cut into squares.

Arkansas Pralines

1 box light brown sugar
1/2 pint whipping cream
1/4 cup butter
1 tablespoon vanilla
2 cups pecan halves

1. In a sauce pan, cook sugar and whipping cream over low to medium heat until soft.
2. Remove from heat, add butter, and cool completely.
3. Stir in vanilla and pecan halves.
4. Beat with a wooden spoon until thickened.
5. Drop on waxed paper with a spoon and let set in refrigerator for about 4 hours or until firm.

Pineapple Upside-Down Pancakes

2 cups flour, sifted
2 teaspoons baking powder
1/2 teaspoon salt
2 cups milk
1 egg
1/3 cup butter, softened
3 tablespoons vegetable oil
1 can crushed pineapples (about 10 ounces)
1 cup brown sugar

1. Mix flour, baking powder, salt, milk, egg, and butter.

2. Heat oil in skillet and pour enough to make single pancakes.

3. After flipping, sprinkle with brown sugar and add crushed pineapples.

4. Serve with your choice of syrup.

Carrot Cake

2 cups flour
2 teaspoons baking powder
1 teaspoon baking soda
1 1/2 teaspoons ground cinnamon
1/4 teaspoon ground nutmeg
1/2 teaspoon salt
3/4 cup vegetable oil
4 large eggs
1 1/2 cups brown sugar
1/2 cup granulated sugar
1/2 cup applesauce
1 teaspoon vanilla extract
3 cups carrots, grated
1 cup vegetable oil

1. Preheat oven to 350°F.
2. In a large mixing bowl, mix together the dry ingredients (flour, baking powder, baking soda, cinnamon, nutmeg, and salt) until well combined. Set aside.
3. In a separate large mixing bowl, use a wire whisk to combine the oil, eggs, brown sugar, granulated sugar, applesauce, and vanilla extract.
4. Mix in the grated carrots.
5. Pour into the dry ingredients and mix with a rubber spatula. Do not overmix.
6. Coat two 9-inch cake pans with nonstick cooking spray and pour equal amounts of batter into each.
7. Bake for 30–35 minutes, or until the tops of cakes are set.

8. Remove from the oven and cool for 20–25 minutes.
9. Remove cake layers from pans and place on wire rack to cool completely. If necessary, use a blunt knife to loosen the layers.
10. Level the top of each cake with a knife. You can scrape or cut across.
11. Place one of the cakes on a cake stand and top with a little over 1/2 cup of the frosting.
12. Smooth the icing into an even layer.
13. Carefully place the other cake on top and frost the top and sides of the cake.
14. Decorate with pecans or flakes of carrot.

Carrot Cake Frosting

Cream cheese (8-ounce block)
1/2 cup butter, unsalted, soft
2 cups powdered sugar
1 teaspoon vanilla extract

1. Using a mixer, beat the cream cheese until smooth.
2. Add the butter and mix for about a minute, or until frosting is well combined and smooth.
3. Add powdered sugar and vanilla extract.
4. Continue mixing until fully combined.

Easy Birthday Cake

2 cups flour
1 1/2 cups whole milk
1 cup granulated sugar
1 cup dark brown sugar
1/2 cup unsweetened cocoa
3/4 cup butter, softened
3 large eggs
2 teaspoons vanilla extract
1 teaspoon baking powder
1 teaspoon baking soda
1/2 teaspoon salt

1. Preheat oven to 350°F.

2. Using a mixer on low speed, combine flour, milk, granulated sugar and dark brown sugar, cocoa, butter, eggs, vanilla extract, baking soda, baking powder, and salt.

3. Increase mixer speed to medium and mix for three minutes.

4. Grease two 8-inch cake pans with vegetable oil.

5. Pour equal amounts of the batter into each pan.

6. Bake for 35 minutes or so. When the cakes are done, a toothpick inserted in the middle will come out dry.

7. Cool in the cake pans for 10 minutes.

8. Invert cake layers onto the wire rack to cool completely. If necessary, use a blunt knife to loosen the layers.

9. Use a serrated knife to level the cake layers.
10. Place a layer on a cake plate and cover the top with a layer of icing.
11. Place the second layer on the first and liberally spread icing over the cake.

Cream Cheese Chocolate Frosting

1/2 cup butter, softened
1 block cream cheese (about 3 ounces)
1 teaspoon vanilla extract
2 cups powdered sugar
2 ounces unsweetened chocolate, melted
2 tablespoons milk

1. Combine all ingredients in a bowl.
2. In a pan, cook mixture over low heat and stir until blended. Do not allow to scorch or boil.
3. Allow to cool and smooth over cake one layer at a time.

Sugar Cookies

1 cup sugar
1 cup shortening
1 cup sour cream
3 eggs, beaten
1 teaspoon vanilla
3 cups flour
1 teaspoon baking powder
1/2 teaspoon salt

1. Preheat oven to 375°F.
2. In a large bowl, combine sugar, shortening, and sour cream.
3. Add eggs and vanilla.
4. Sift flour, baking powder, and salt together.
5. Add to cream mixture and blend well.
6. Chill about 2 hours.
7. Roll out to a 1/2-inch-thick layer. Cut out using a cookie cutter or glass.
8. Place on a well-greased cookie sheet.
9. Sprinkle with sugar.
10. Bake for 15 minutes, or until light brown.

Aunt Greeley's Tea Cakes

4 cups flour
2 1/2 cups sugar
2 teaspoons salt
3/4 teaspoon baking soda
1 1/2 cups shortening
2 eggs

1. Preheat oven to 375°F.

2. Mix flour, sugar, salt, baking soda, shortening, and eggs. The mixture will be thick.

3. Roll into walnut-size balls and then flatten with a fork.

4. Bake for 12 minutes, or until brown around the edges.

Leftovers

How come the turkey sandwich was better than the turkey?

No one knows. It might just be one of the mysteries of life.

Raymond J's Big Turkey Sandwich

Didn't have turkey? You can use brisket, chicken, or ham with (shudder) instant stuffing.

2 large slices wheat bread
2 teaspoons cranberry sauce
3 tablespoons dressing
2 teaspoons gravy, warm
3 thick slices turkey (white and dark meat)
2 lettuce leaves
Sliced dill pickles
2 slices tomato
1 teaspoon mustard
1 teaspoon mayonnaise
salt and pepper to taste

1. Toast bread to medium dark.

2. Spread cranberry sauce on one slice of bread.

3. Layer sandwich with dressing, warm gravy, turkey, lettuce, pickles, and tomato.

    Layering keeps the sandwich from slipping around.

4. Add salt and pepper.

5. Spread mustard and mayonnaise on second slice and place on top of sandwich.

6. Use toothpicks on opposite corners to hold sandwich together and slice diagonally.

7. Serve with chips, soup, or salad. Most likely chips.

Turkey Salad

2 cups diced cooked turkey or chicken
1/4 cup celery, diced
2 tablespoons onion, minced
1/2 cup walnuts, chopped
2 tablespoons pimentos
1/2 teaspoon salt
4 hard-boiled eggs, chopped
1/2 cup sweet pickle relish

1. Combine meat, celery, onion, walnuts, pimentos, salt, eggs, and relish.

2. Mix well.

3. Serve on bread or with crackers.

Easy Dinner in a Skillet

This is one of the easy recipes that make it look as though you were doing something fancy.

1 1/2 pounds ground beef or turkey
1 medium onion, chopped
1 can green beans (8–10 ounces)
1 can whole kernel corn (8–10 ounces)
1 small jar mushrooms (4–6 ounces)
1 can cheddar cheese soup (8–10 ounces)
1/2 cup green onions, chopped
salt and pepper to taste
1 package cornbread mix

1. Preheat oven to at 350°F.
2. Mix salt and pepper to ground meat.
3. In a skillet brown the ground meat.
4. Drain cans of vegetables and add to skillet.
5. Then add mushrooms, cheese soup, and green onions.
6. Place in pan or casserole dish.
7. Separately, following the instructions on box to make cornbread batter. Pour batter over meat and vegetable mixture.
8. Bake in oven for 45 minute or until cornbread is golden brown.

Turkey Gumbo Soup

4 tablespoons olive oil
4 tablespoons butter
4 tablespoons flour
1/4 cup garlic, chopped or sliced
1/4 cup onion, chopped
sprig of parsley
1 bell pepper, chopped
1 cup okra, chopped
1 can stewed tomatoes (15–20 ounces)
1/4 cup Worcestershire sauce
3 cups cooked turkey, diced
3 cups cooked ham, diced (optional)
3 pounds shrimp or crab, fresh or frozen (optional)
Cooked rice

1. In a large pot, make a roux from the oil, butter, and flour.

2. Cook over low heat, stirring constantly, until brown.

3. Add garlic, onion, parsley, and bell pepper. Cook until tender, about 10 minutes.

4. Add okra, tomatoes, and Worcestershire sauce. Cook for several minutes before adding turkey, ham, and/or seafood.

5. If gumbo is thin, add a mixture of 1 tablespoon of flour and 3 tablespoons of vegetable oil to thicken.

6. Serve over cooked rice.

It's a Party

Have fun.

Want your holiday gathering to go right? Remember to incorporate fun. After people arrive, they greet and hug (and sometimes, argue about nothing). Then they offer to help you in the kitchen or prepare whatever dishes they brought.

Why not get people started with a few games? Or you can save the games for after for those who are not in a food coma.

This section includes a few games you can play.

Suggested Games
- Dominoes
- Hearts
- Spades
- Bridge
- Charades
- Pictionary
- Family Fued
- 20 Questions
- Scavenger hunts (cell phone pictures)

About the Author

Wilma was born in Newport, Arkansas. She attended Branch High, a segregated school, and completed her degree at Arkansas Baptist College in Little Rock, Arkansas. She married Raymond J. Miller soon after graduation.

While working nights and raising children, she perfected her recipes at home, at family reunions, and at church events.

Even after the death of her husband to heart disease and daughter to cancer, Wilma has not slowed down at all. Late in life, she started a new career as a caregiver and author. Wilma is also a performance artist specializing in religious comedy.

Momma's Home Cooking was her first book; this is her second.

You can learn more about Wilma, get recipes, and sign up for her newsletter at http://www.wilmajeanmiller.com.

Made in the USA
Middletown, DE
31 January 2019